# TEEN TIME

THIS BOOK IS ABOUT WHAT TEENAGERS GO THROUGH DURING THEIR TEENAGE YEARS. MANY FACTORS AFFECT THEM DURING THESE CRUCIAL YEARS OF LIFE BECAUSE IT CHANGES THEM AS A PERSON AND EMBEDS THAT IN THEIR PERSON

DEVANG ASHISH KHAKHAR

ISBN 979-888591202-0

INDEX

# Contents

## Chapter 1: Early Teen

Puberty and adolescence are two terms interlinked to each other representing certain changes and period of such changes. Puberty refers to the physical changes leading to sexual maturity in a boy or a girl. Adolescence refers to the transition period when psychological and social changes take place in a boy or girl. Puberty is the reason for the adolescence and this period may vary from one person to another.

Stages of Adolescence:

- Early Adolescence (Ages 10 to 13):
- During this stage, children often start to grow more quickly. They also begin notice other body changes, including hair growth under the arms and near the genitals, breast development in females and enlargement of the testicles in males. They usually start a year or two earlier in girls than boys, and it can be normal for some changes to start as early as age 8 for females and age 9 for males. Many girls may start their period at around age 12, on average 2-3 years after the

onset of breast development.

- These body changes can inspire curiosity and anxiety in some—especially if they do not know what to expect or what is normal. Some children may also question their gender identity at this time, and the onset of puberty can be a difficult time for transgender children.
- Early adolescents have concrete, black-and-white thinking. Things are either right or wrong, great, or terrible, without much room in between. It is normal at this stage for young people to centre their thinking on themselves (called "egocentrism"). As part of this, preteens and early teens are often self-conscious about their appearance and feel as though they are always being judged by their peers.
- Pre-teens feel an increased need for privacy. They may start to explore ways of being independent from their family. In this process, they may push boundaries and may react strongly if parents or guardians reinforce limits.

- Middle Adolescence (Ages 14 to 17):

- Physical changes from puberty continue during middle adolescence. Most males will have started their growth spurt, and puberty-related changes continue. They may have some voice cracking, for example, as their voices lower. Some develop acne. Physical changes may be nearly complete for females, and most girls now have regular periods.
- At this age, many teens become interested in romantic and sexual relationships. They may question and explore their sexual identity—which may be stressful if they do not have support from peers, family, or

community. Another typical way of exploring sexuality for teens of all genders is self-stimulation, also called masturbation.

- Many middle adolescents have more arguments with their parents as they struggle for more independence. They may spend less time with family and more time with friends. They are very concerned about their appearance, and peer pressure may peak at this age.
- The brain continues to change and mature in this stage, but there are still many differences in how a normal middle adolescent think compared to an adult. Much of this is because the frontal lobes are the last areas of the brain to mature—development is not complete until a person is well into their 20s! The frontal lobes play a big role in coordinating complex decision making, impulse control, and being able to consider multiple options and consequences. Middle adolescents are more able to think abstractly and consider "the big picture," but they still may lack the ability to apply it in the moment. For example, in certain situations, kids in middle adolescence may find themselves thinking things like:

    - *"I'm doing well enough in math, and I really want to see this movie... one night of skipping studying won't matter."*
    - *"Marijuana is legal now, so it can't be that bad."*

While they may be able to walk through the logic of avoiding risks outside of these situations, strong emotions often continue to drive their decisions when impulses come into play.

- Late Adolescents (Ages 18-21 and beyond!):

Late adolescents generally have completed physical development and grown to their full adult height. They usually have more impulse control by now and may be better able to gauge risks and rewards accurately. In comparison to middle adolescents, youth in late adolescence might find themselves thinking:

- *"While I do love Paul Rudd movies, I need to study for my final."*
- *"I should wear a condom...even though my girlfriend is on birth control, that's not 100% in preventing pregnancy."*
- *"Even though marijuana is legal, I'm worried about how it might affect my mood and work/school performance."*

Teens entering early adulthood have a stronger sense of their own individuality now and can identify their own values. They may become more focused on the future and base decisions on their hopes and ideals. Friendships and romantic relationships become more stable. They become more emotionally and physically separated from their family. However, many re-establish an "adult" relationship with their parents, considering them more an equal from whom to ask advice and discuss mature topics with, rather than an authority figure.

Changes in the Brain and Behaviour during adolescence

Adolescence — the transition from childhood to adulthood — is a time of great change in the brain and behaviour. In addition to sexual maturity, individuals also develop social and emotional skills during this time that will serve them as adults. Traditionally, researchers trying to understand this period have focused on a mismatch in the brain between increased sensitivity to rewarding stimuli and still-developing inhibitory control, which appears to lead to vulnerability to psychiatric disorders and risky behaviour such as drug-seeking. What follows is a discussion of how hormones, the brain, and social factors affect adolescent development.

Puberty also describes the transition from childhood to adulthood, but it focuses specifically on changes in physiology and behaviour. These changes differ between the sexes and include mating behaviours, secondary sex characteristics, and activation of hormonal crosstalk between the brain and the gonads or sex organs. Scientists who investigate these changes often ask whether brain and behaviour changes observed during adolescence depend on puberty. They have found that some do, and some do not.

Research in both humans and model organisms indicates adolescents are more sensitive to rewarding stimuli than adults. Biological sex also appears to play a role. For instance, scientists have shown that human males are more impulsive than females through their mid-twenties and that adolescent male rats are more sensitive to tasty food than both adolescent female and adult rats. At least some of these observations may be explained by recent studies demonstrating the cortex and the striatum, the part of the brain thought to play a large role in determining how rewarding a stimulus or behaviour is, develop more slowly in males than in females.

The circuit that plays a large role in receiving and regulating rewarding stimuli is the mesocorticolimbic dopamine pathway. In rodents and primates, this pathway undergoes extensive changes during adolescence. One of the most striking changes is the steady, linear increase in dopaminergic neural projections that happens in both males and females in the brain area known as the medial prefrontal cortex, or m PFC. In addition to the increase in projections, the brain regions involved in this circuit also increase the expression of dopamine receptors during adolescence.

In attempting to understand the interplay between hormones and brain development, scientists have found a specific role for puberty on the m PFC. For instance, this brain region undergoes neuronal pruning and a corresponding decrease in volume during puberty, but not in female rats that have had their ovaries removed and are thus missing crucial hormones. Researchers now suspect that changes in structure that happen in the m PFC during puberty could be a driver of the differences in decision-making and reward learning between adolescence and adulthood, but further studies are needed to fully understand this potential link.

Alongside changes in the brain and hormones, adolescent humans, and rodents experience changes in how they respond to social structure that can, in turn, drive changes in neural circuitry. In humans, adolescents start to rely more on their peers for social support and, in doing so, learn behaviours that will serve them as adults. Reward circuitry, particularly the region known as the basolateral amygdala, is known to be involved in how the brain responds to social situations. Another area, the medial amygdala, which is outside of the traditional reward circuit, has provided researchers with some understanding of how sex differences affect the brain's response to social reward.

The experts studying adolescence have begun to identify overarching themes. First, sex differences during adolescence may be a precursor to sex differences in responses to reward during adulthood. Second, the mesocorticolimbic dopamine pathway is the brain circuit that is essential for changes to how the brain perceives social interactions and reward during adolescence. Finally, both hormones and environmental factors, such as peer relationships and exchanges, drive changes to this circuitry, which can be sensitive to drugs of abuse and social stress. More research is needed, as scientists are only beginning to understand how the brain, hormones, and environment affect reward during adolescence.

Emotional Development milestones:

- Increased ability to interact with peers
- Increased ability to engage in competition
- Developing and testing values and beliefs that will guide present and future behaviours
- Has a strong group identity; increasingly defines self through peers
- Acquiring a sense of accomplishment based upon the achievement of greater physical strength and self-control
- Defines self-concept in part by success in school.

Intellectual/Cognitive Development milestones:

- Early adolescents have an increased ability to learn and apply skills.
- The early adolescent years mark the beginning of abstract thinking but revert to concrete thought under stress.
- Even though abstract thinking generally starts during this age period, preteens are still developing this method of reasoning and are not able to make all intellectual leaps, such as inferring a motive or reasoning hypothetically.
- Youth in this age range learn to extend their way of thinking beyond their personal experiences and knowledge and start to view the world outside of an absolute black, white/right-wrong perspective.
- Interpretative ability develops during the years of early adolescence, as does the ability to recognize cause and

affect sequences.

Emotional Changes

Most experts believe that the idea of young teens being controlled by their "raging hormones" is exaggerated.

Nonetheless, this age can be one of mood swings, sulking, a craving for privacy and short tempers.

Young children are not able to think far ahead, but young teens can and do—which allows them to worry about the future.

Some may worry excessively about:

★ their school performance.

★ their appearance, physical development, and popularity.

★ the possible death of a parent.

★ being bullied at school.

★ school violence

★ not having friends

★ drugs and drinking

★ hunger and poverty in the country

★ their inability to get a good job

★ the divorce of their parents; and

★ dying.

Many young teens are very self-conscious. And, because they are experiencing dramatic physical and emotional changes, they are often overly sensitive about themselves. They may worry about personal qualities or "defects" that are major to them but are hardly noticeable to others. (Belief: "I can't go to the party tonight because everyone will laugh at this baseball sized zit on my forehead." Facts: The pimple is tiny and hidden by hair.)

Teens' emotions often seem exaggerated. Their actions seem inconsistent. It is normal for young teens to swing regularly from being happy to being sad and from feeling smart to feeling dumb. In fact, some think of adolescence as a second toddlerhood.

As Carol Bleifield, a middle school counsellor in Wisconsin, explains, “One minute, they want to be treated and taken care of like a small child. Five minutes later they are pushing adults away, saying, ‘Let me do it.’ It may help if you can help them understand that they are amid some major changes, changes that don’t always move steadily ahead.” In addition to changes in the emotions that they feel, most young teens explore different ways to express their emotions. For example, a child who greeted friends and visitors with enthusiastic hugs may turn into a teen who gives these same people only a small wave or nod of the head. Similarly, hugs and kisses for a parent may be replaced with a pulling away and an “Oh, Mom!” It’s important to remember, though, that these are usually changes in ways of expressing feelings and not the actual feelings about friends, parents, and family.

Cognitive Changes:

The cognitive or mental, changes that take place in early adolescence may be less easy to see, but they can be just as dramatic as physical and emotional changes. During adolescence, most teens make large leaps in the way they think, reason, and learn. Younger children need to see and touch things to be convinced that they are real. But in early adolescence, children become able to think about ideas and about things that they can’t see or touch.

They become better able to think though problems and see the consequences of different points of view or actions. For the first time, they can think about what might be, instead of what is.

A 6-yearold thinks a smiling person is happy and a crying person is sad. A 14-year-old may tell you that a sad person smiles to hide his true feelings. The cognitive changes allow young teens to learn more advanced and complicated material in school. They become eager to gain and apply knowledge and to consider a range of ideas or options.

These mental changes also carry over into their emotional lives. Within the family, for example, the ability to reason may change the way a young teen talks to and acts around her parents. She begins to anticipate how her parents will react to something she says or does and prepares an answer or an explanation.

In addition, these mental changes lead adolescents to consider who they are and who they may be. This is a process called identity formation and it is a major activity during adolescence. Most adolescents will explore a range of possible identities.

They go through "phases" that to a parent can seem to be ever-changing. Indeed, adolescents who don't go through this period of exploration are at greater risk of developing psychological problems, especially depression, when they are adults. Just as adults, who with more experience and cognitive maturity can struggle with their different roles, adolescents struggle in developing a sense of who they are. They begin to realize that they play different roles with different people: son or daughter, friend, teammate, student, worker and so forth.

Young teens may be able to think more like adults, but they still do not have the experience that is needed to act like adults. As a result, their behaviour may be out of step with their ideas. For example, your child may participate eagerly in a walk to raise money to save the environment—but litter the route she walks with soda cans.

Or she may spend an evening on the phone or exchanging e-mails with a friend talking about how they dislike a classmate because she gossips. It takes time for young teens and their parents to adjust to all these changes. But the changes are also exciting. They allow a young teen to see what she can be like in the future and to develop plans for becoming that person.

# II

## Chapter 2: Middle Adolescence

Mid-adolescence is one of the sub-stages that we go through humans after childhood and before adulthood. It is a crucial stage for the development of complex psychological processes such as identity, and it is itself a period in which significant changes occur on a biological and social level.

General characteristics of middle adolescence

Mid adolescence is characterized by a concern for reconcile personal and external recognition. While the first stage of recognition is based on physical or bodily exploration, in the second there is a particular psychological concern, which manifests itself in the search for emotional bonds and the acceptance of the peer group.

Due to the above, the main reference group and even psychological security, ceases to be family and begins to focus on friendly or emotional bonds with peers.

It is a fundamental process for the development of autonomy, individual responsibility, and identity, as well as for the development of complex cognitive processes such as symbolization, generalization, and abstraction, which allow to establish a broader view of the world.

This also forms the basis of much of the concern at this point, in fact, romantic relationships usually begin to consolidate at this point, around shared experiences and interests.

Finally, intergenerational relations are a key element, because they make it possible to consolidate the identification process through establish complementary or antagonistic differences between themselves and members of different groups.

Some psychological elements:

We summarize below some of the specific elements surrounding mid-adolescence, particularly at the psychosocial level, the middle of adolescence is characterized mainly by a concern for personal-social affirmation, which includes certain elements that we will see below:

- Differentiation of the family group.
- Parental grief following the loss of the desired child.
- **I want to assert sexual and social appeal.**
- Emergence of sexual impulses.
- Exploration of personal skills.
- Social concern and for new activities.
- Challenging previous positions.

Characteristics of Neuronal, Cognitive and Psychological Maturation:

As we have said, adolescence is characterized by the manifestation of changes on a biological as well as psychological and social level.

- Growth of the prefrontal cortex, which relates to influencing social issues and developing problem-solving skills.

- Cognitive skills such as the development of abstract thinking (although there is concrete thinking in stressful situations); and a better understanding of the consequences of acts, with a particular concern for oneself.
- **Body image development.**
- Development of impractical or improbable projects.
- Meaningful sense of empowerment.

Time Management during middle adolescence

Time management is a complex skill. Today's youth have many more demands on their time than their parents did when they were teens themselves. Competition in school and sports has increased. New communication technologies provide a vast array of ways to socialize. The Internet provides an infinite supply of information and unlimited choices. Inexpensive entertainment is readily available with just a click of a button. Therefore, youth must learn to budget and to manage their time in a way that allows them to balance competing needs and priorities: work (e.g., schoolwork, employment, chores), recreation (entertainment and fun), relaxation (sleep, rest), relationships (family and friends), and self-care (exercise, diet, hygiene, grooming). Clearly, youths' ability to effectively manage their time is an essential skill they will need throughout their lives.

Parents can begin to help adolescents develop this skill by having high (but attainable) expectations for school achievement, household chores, and other important activities. Furthermore, parents should clearly communicate these expectations, and regularly reinforce them. For example, parents should make it clear that they expect their teens to attend school every day, complete homework on time, perform regular weekly chores, and participate in at least one extracurricular activity or part-time job to continue to receive privileges such as television and gaming time, going out with friends, having cell phone minutes, etc. These expectations teach youth to responsibly prioritize their time and create structured activities that challenge their physical, mental, social, and emotional growth. Youth should not be permitted to have an abundance of unstructured, free time as they often become bored when they are idle and can too quickly find negative activities to fill their time.

Meanwhile, activities which do little to promote physical, mental, social, or emotional growth need to be limited. Parents will need to establish time limits for purely recreational activities and specify the conditions that must be met to engage in these activities. For instance, parents may decide that one hour of television or video games are permitted each day, but homework must be completed first; or texting and chatting is permitted before 10PM but only if grades remain above a C. Furthermore, parents may wish to consider if there are any prohibited types of games, television shows, movies, Internet sites etc. If so, parents should establish clear rules about these limitations. There is quite a lot of media targeting teen audiences that depicts graphic violence and sexual imagery, or may contain other negative, offensive, or distasteful content.

Although parents should limit unstructured idle time, it remains important for youth to have some relaxation and "down" time; the key is moderation, as is the type and quality of relaxation activities. Sedentary, passive activities can steal away time from other more healthy and enriching activities such as physical activities, face-to-face socialization, and family time. Youth should be encouraged to find pleasure and enjoyment in activities that enrich their lives, e.g., reading, crafting, athletics, cooking, photography, woodworking, etc. Developing an interest in these activities at an early age may lead to a lifetime of satisfaction and enjoyment.

Decisions about how youth spend their time should include input from both teens and their parents. To establish realistic and reasonable limits on passive recreation, families with teens should sit down together and discuss the various time commitments and existing family schedules (school, work, chores, sports, clubs, and time for relationships with family and friends). This approach helps youth to establish priorities for their time and to make wise choices about they wish to spend their "free" time.

Family Commitments

Family rules should also establish clear expectations about the responsibilities of family members toward each other. Families will want to decide how much time is spent together in both planned and unplanned activities. For example, the Stephens family may require that family members share 5 meals together every week, designate one night per week as family activity night (movie night, game night, etc), and one "evening in" when everyone is at home, even if everyone is doing their own activities. For some families, work and school schedules vary week to week making this sort of planning difficult. However, even these families can designate one night per week when family members sit down together and review the upcoming week's schedule, and then decide upon which night will be family game night, which meals will be shared, and which evening everyone is expected to be "in."

Many youths will protest these family rules. At this age, it may simply be more appealing to go out with friends every night; however, these rules are beneficial. First, these rules help teens to establish a lifetime pattern of maintaining a strong commitment and allegiance to their families. Second, family members need to spend time together if they wish to have a relationship with each other. Strong relationships between children and their parents, and between siblings, are built by spending time together. These multiple relationships within families help to strengthen youths' resilience, because it means there is more than one person to turn to when they are upset, lonely, or need guidance. Third, when parents make it a priority to spend time with their children, these actions communicate to their children that they are loved and valued. Finally, spending time together as a family improves the communication skills of family members as they learn to respectfully resolve disputes and disagreements while valuing and appreciating each person's worth. These communication skills will become important interpersonal skills and serve to reduce problems such as disrespectful language and oppositional behaviours.

While it is important to establish rules about spending time together, it is also important to establish family rules about time spent apart. These rules ensure everyone's safety. It is reasonable for parents to insist they be kept informed about the physical location of their teens, which friends and/or adults are at that location, and what activity their teens are doing at that location. Not only do parents need to know how to find their children in event of an emergency, but when teens are expected to regularly communicate about what they are doing, with whom, and where, it reduces the likelihood of them engaging in activities that are dangerous or will otherwise get them into trouble. Many youths will be opposed to constantly checking in with their parents. However, this opposition can be lessened if parents reciprocate the courtesy. For instance, if mom is going to be late getting home from work, she can call the kids and let them know she's going to be late and why. Or, if dad was running errands but then decided to stop by a friend's home to watch some football, he can call the family and inform them of this change of plans. Thus, the rule about keeping family members informed about each other's whereabouts applies to everyone equally.

It's also appropriate for youth to have curfews on both school nights and weekends. At the very least, family curfews should coincide with the local laws regarding teen curfews, but these family rules should also consider what time frames will enable youth to balance for their social needs with their obligations to academics, athletics, work, family, and their own health requirements for sufficient rest and exercise.

Socializing, Dating during middle adolescence

Family rules and expectations can become complicated when teens visit each other's homes. As discussed, every family has their own values and beliefs, and their own rules that reflect these values and beliefs. Parents of different families often see their roles differently. These differing expectations can become sources of difficulty for teens and their parents. Nevertheless, parents need to establish clear guidelines that enable their youth to make wise choices.

First, youth should be explicitly taught they are expected to follow their own family's rules whether they are at home or visiting someone else's home; and they must also comply with the rules of the home they are visiting. However, these two sets of rules may conflict with each other (i.e., one set of rules is more strict or more lenient than the other) leaving teens to judge which set of rules should apply. Teens should be instructed to follow the stricter set of rules when they are in doubt.

The best way parents can help prevent problems from developing is to be in direct communication with other parents. Before youth visit each other's homes, the children's parents should talk with each other, on the phone or in person, so they can become acquainted and begin a dialogue about rules and expectations. If one parent has strong convictions about certain rules or behaviour that should be enforced regardless of which home a child is visiting, they need to respectfully discuss these expectations with the other parent to see if their expectations are agreeable to the other parent. When there is disagreement, parents should discuss their different approaches and work out a satisfactory solution. For example, if Johnny's mom doesn't want Johnny hanging out at a friend's house without adult supervision, Johnny's mom can discuss this with Ken's mom and inquire whether there will be an adult present during the time the two boys are planning to visit. If Ken's mother reports she doesn't share that belief or that she can't be home when the guys want to socialize, Johnny's mom may ask that the boys visit at her home instead (with her supervision) for the afternoon or the boys may need to reschedule their visit to coincide with a time when Ken's mom is expected to be home.

If parents become aware of activities or rules at another child's home that they do not agree with, they should calmly discuss their concerns with the parents of the other child. Perhaps the youth did not accurately explain the difference in rules or perhaps the other parents were not aware of the reasons for concern. If after that conversation, parents feel like the friends' parents do not see the need to address the behaviours or to adjust their monitoring or rule application, parents may need to create other ways youth can still foster that friendship without socializing at that friend's house. As mentioned, teens can be taught a simple "default" rule to follow: When two sets of rules conflict, follow the stricter version of the two rules. Then, at the soonest opportunity the youth should discuss the conflicting rules with their own parents.

Adolescents also begin dating during this time and may begin to form romantic/sexual relationships. Parents should first discuss with each other their own thoughts about dating, and values regarding sexually active teens, and teens should be made aware of any expectations their parents have.

Driving privileges

Consistent with laws that apply to everyone, parents should help their youth recognize that driving is a privilege and not a right. As such, it is a privilege that is earned, and can be taken away. Similarly, the use of a car, whether the family car or a teen's own car, is an expensive privilege that can be awarded for responsible behaviour or taken away for irresponsible behaviour. At a minimum parents should clearly establish and communicate their expectations about driving and the use of a car. Specifically, teens should be aware of what behaviour will result in the loss of driving privileges (for instance, drug or alcohol use).

Experimentation with alcohol, tobacco, and other drugs

Besides talking to youth about the risks to using substances, parents need to express clear rules and expectations around teen substance use. At a minimum parents should establish rules that are consistent with state and federal laws. Youth should not be allowed to smoke or use any tobacco product before they turn 18, and they shouldn't be allowed to drink until they are 21. Illegal drugs are off-limits for the same reasons; because in fact, they are illegal. Parents need to make these boundaries clear. Therefore, parents should not provide their youth with alcohol or tobacco or allow any youth to use alcohol or tobacco while in their presence. Some parents may wish to make an exception for substances used during sacred religious events or important family traditions. For instance, in the Catholic tradition, the consumption of a small amount of wine is part of a holy sacrament and in the Lakota tradition, tobacco may be consumed during a sweat lodge purification ceremony.

Furthermore, youth should clearly understand what the consequences are for illicit drug use (including alcohol), such as the loss of driving privileges, and establish clear guidelines about what should be done if they are with friends who are using alcohol and other drugs. It is important that parents make it clear, that not only do they expect their own children to refrain from alcohol or other drug use, but youth are expected to avoid being with friends while those friends are using alcohol or other drugs.

Mental, Emotional, and Behavioural Healthcare for Adolescents

As mentioned, adolescence is a period of rapid growth. But this growth is not limited to their bodies. Adolescents also experience rapid cognitive development, emotional development, and social development.

Therefore, annual physical exams should also be screening adolescents for behavioural health concerns such as depression; anxiety; or possible problems with tobacco, alcohol, and other drugs.

In fact, the American Academy of Paediatrics recommends that teens receive an annual depression screening at their routine physical check-up. If a doctor suspects that a youth may be struggling with an emotional problem or has a problem with substance use, the doctor can refer the family to a behavioural healthcare specialist for treatment.

Parents have an important role in identifying the early warning signs of a behavioural or emotional problem because they regularly observe their teens' behavioural and emotional patterns.

If parents have observed any changes in mood or behaviour that lasts more than a week or two and that is starting to affect the youth's ability to perform daily activities such as school or work, or if parents notice a change in their youth's enjoyment of social or recreational activities, these changes could signal a developing problem.

Here are some examples of behavioural and emotional symptoms that should be reported to the healthcare provider:

- A mood that is frequently sad, tearful, sullen, irritable, or angry
- A lack of attention to physical hygiene (bathing, brushing teeth, etc.)
- A loss of interest in activities that were previously enjoyable
- Withdrawal from family and friends, becoming socially isolated
- A loss of motivation; for instance, difficulty completing schoolwork and chores, or difficulty with their employer
- A significant decline in academic performance

- Frequently getting into trouble at school or frequent arguments with parents and sibling
- Changes in sleep habits: sleeping a great deal more than usual and still being tired; or sleeping a great deal less than usual and seeming energized despite the lack of sleep
- Changes in eating habits: a sudden loss of appetite or sudden increase in appetite,
- Frequent physical aches and pains that cannot be easily explained: headaches, migraines, stomach aches, back pain, etc.
- The smell of alcohol, or a chemical smell that parents do not recognize

Any of the above symptoms could indicate that a youth is struggling with some type of behavioural health problem such as depression, anxiety, drug use, or an eating disorder. Adolescence is a time of many significant changes, and teens must deal with many situations each day that can cause a noticeable change in emotional responses. It is understandable that parents may feel confused when trying to distinguish between normal teenage behaviour and unusual behaviour that may indicate a more significant problem. Nonetheless, parents should be concerned about a teen who experiences sadness or irritability more days than not.

The symptoms mentioned above should not be dismissed as "just a phase," or "just part of being a teenager."

If parents notice any of these symptoms or have any doubts about whether their teen's behaviours or moods are signs of a larger problem, they should discuss these concerns with a qualified healthcare professional.

When parents muster the courage to talk to their teen's healthcare providers about their concerns for their child's emotional welfare, this communicates to the teen that emotional health is just as important as physical health.

Once healthcare providers become aware of these concerns, they can refer the teen and his family to the appropriate treatment services in their community

Mental, Emotional, and Behavioural- II

In addition to the general symptoms listed previously, some behavioural health concerns have very specific warning signs. Eating disorders may be indicated by significant changes in eating behaviours such as: binging on very large amounts of food; hiding food in personal spaces such as the bedroom; avoiding food or activities in which everyone is eating; developing unusual rituals around food such as cutting everything into tiny pieces and then eating a specific number of pieces; immediately using the restroom after meals (to purge), or extreme amounts of exercise.

Youth who are struggling with an anxiety disorder can seem anxious most of the time. They may constantly worry that something bad is going to happen; that they will fail, make a mistake, or do something horridly embarrassing; or they may anticipate the worst possible outcome. These youth may begin to avoid situations or circumstances where they anticipate these negative experiences will occur such as avoiding parties for fear of embarrassment or quitting the debate team because they are certain they will make a mistake and disappoint their teammates. They may become so worried or nervous that they avoid going to school or feel unable to leave the safety of their home for fear of what might happen. Other anxious youth may feel like they constantly need to check and re-check things like making sure the front door is locked or checking to see if they remembered to put their homework into their backpack. Sometimes anxious youth may experience panic attacks that seem to just "come out of the blue." People who experience panic attacks describe feeling like they can't breathe, or that their heart is racing, and experience intense fear. Panic attacks are a symptom of several different types of anxiety disorders.

Troubled youth often develop problems with alcohol and other drugs, but even seemingly happy and well-adjusted children can develop drug use problems. If youth come home smelling like alcohol, smoke, or another chemical-like smell the parents don't recognize, it could indicate that they are using the substances that cause those smells or are hanging out with other youth who do. Conversely, some youth may come home smelling too nice. Their breath may be too minty-fresh, or their clothes smell like a bottle of Febreze®. This could also indicate they are trying to cover up or to remove the smells of alcohol, tobacco, or drugs. Furthermore, if youth appear to have impaired mental or physical functioning, this can also be a serious indication they are using substances. Impaired functioning may be indicated by slurred speech; difficulty maintaining a sensible conversation with others; difficulty remaining on task; stumbling, falling, or other balance difficulties; or appearing to be disconnected from everyone else.

Many teens with substance use problems try very hard to hide their substance use from their parents; so, even if the parents do not observe their child's impaired functioning, they may notice their child becoming much more secretive about their activities and their friends, and they may begin to avoid their home and family much more than usual. If parents or healthcare providers suspect a youth is using drugs, blood tests can be ordered to check for substances in the child's system. However, these tests may not tell the whole story since they can usually only detect drugs used within the last 72 hours. However, alcohol can only be detected within a few hours of use, while marijuana may be detected for nearly a month after use. For these reasons, some parents may choose to bypass the doctor's office and use the over-the-counter drug tests available online and in many drug stores.

Depression is another behavioural health concern that affects youth. Unfortunately, many people mistakenly dismiss a teen's "moodiness" as just a normal part of adolescent development, and therefore teens with depression do not receive the treatment they need. According to the National Institute of Mental Health, only 1 in 3 teens with depression receive the treatment that they need and therefore, they unnecessarily suffer and struggle on their own. While a depressed mood on most days may indicate depression, frequent anger and irritability can also indicate a depressive disorder, as can changes in appetite, changes in sleep, and a disregard for basic hygiene and personal appearance. Parents should be alert to these symptoms and if they have concerns, they should discuss this with their child's healthcare provider.

Teen Suicide

A primary symptom of depression is a sense of hopelessness. Sometimes when youth feel this kind of deep despair, they begin to consider suicide as a solution to end their suffering. But depression is not the only cause of teen suicides. Most suicides are completed under the influence of alcohol and other drugs placing teens that use alcohol and drugs at greater risk. Many suicides are impulsive in nature, while others occur after a great deal of planning and thought. Victims of bullying, and victims of abuse are at risk, as are teens that feel isolated and lonely. In short, there is no one single cause for the disturbing problem of teen suicide. In fact, suicide is the second leading cause of death in young people aged 15-24.

Parents should be on the look-out for possible warning signs that their child may be at risk for suicide. First, youth who are struggling with any emotional or behavioural problems, and/or who use alcohol and other drugs, have an increased risk for suicide. More specifically, parents should take seriously ANY comments their children make about wanting to die or wanting to kill themselves. Comments like, "I'd be better off dead," "I'll just kill myself," "No one would miss me if I were gone," "I wonder what it would be like to die" should ALWAYS be taken seriously. These comments may be made verbally, or these kinds of comments may be written in a journal, an email, a text message, or a website posting (such as Facebook®). While some youth indicate they are considering suicide by making direct comments about death and dying, other youth may be more indirect: making a will, planning their funeral, or giving away beloved possessions. A frequently missed indicator of an eminent suicide is when a previously depressed person suddenly begins to feel better, has more energy, and seems to have miraculously turned the corner. Their loved ones may be relieved to see such remarkable improvement. But this "improvement" may be since once a depressed person has made the decision to attempt suicide, and begins to plan a suicide, they begin to feel better, more at peace, knowing that an end to their suffering is now in sight.

If parents notice any of these symptoms, they should immediately reach out to their child and seek professional help. Many parents are reluctant to discuss suicide with their teens for fear that such a discussion will only worsen a bad situation; but usually people considering suicide are relieved to release this secret burden and want to be helped. Suicidal thoughts are often accompanied by the belief that no one cares about them or understands their pain. When parents initiate such a discussion, they are communicating that they do care, and want to understand what their child is experiencing.

If parents suspect their youth is in immediate danger, they should not leave the child alone and should escort the child to the nearest emergency room.

# III

## Chapter 3: Young adult

Late adolescence is when things start to stabilize, and we begin navigating life on our own terms for the first time. We graduate high school and explore who we are in the world as we leave home, move to new cities, decide whether to go to college and start learning how to live on our own.

The late adolescence is the last stage in the development of adolescence. It occurs between the ages of 17 and 19 and is a moment of settlement of all the changes experienced throughout this vital period. Little by little, the adolescent recovers the balance lost with the onset of puberty, the result of the acceptance and integration of all the physical, emotional, and psychological changes experienced. This recovery of balance is necessary to start the transition to adult life in a state of healthy at all levels. At times, entering adulthood with certain unresolved imbalances will be the cause of social maladjustments that will manifest themselves in the medium and long term.

### Characteristics of late adolescence

The adolescent, during this stage, manages to create a personal identity (the result of the integration of his previous being with his new and free personal choices), create new social relationships and internalize moral and ethical values that will determine his progressive entry and functioning in the adult world.

Thought reaches the level of formal operations, which allows it to carry out all a series of cognitive operations with which it will evolve in this last stage of adolescent development.

Physical changes in late adolescence

The physical changes produced in adolescence are much more intense during the first stage. In late adolescence, there is a progressive deceleration of growth. In this way, hormonal secretions, growth, and body changes (height, weight, bone mass, etc.), the development of organs and systems (sexual maturation, growth of different organs), etc. they stop their progression due to the maturity reached.

At this stage, the following changes take place:

- the final height of male adolescents, which can be extended to 21 years (in the case of female adolescents, the final height is established during middle adolescence)
- brain development continues to develop, completing its maturation between 25-30 years
- emotional control is achieved in this last period of the adolescent
- the peak of bone mass acquisition is reached.

Psychological changes in late adolescence

The most prominent psychological changes in this stage of adolescence occur about independence, body image, friends, and identity:

- Independence: after the hard process of de-identification with parental values and the possible conflicts that occur during the early and middle stages, these values are re-accepted but from a place of personal construction of their own.
- Body image: the changes experienced since the beginning of adolescence produce insecurity and comparisons with respect to one's personal image. During this stage, they can accept the changes and the result, a new personal image with which they identify and accept.
- Friendships: adolescence begins with a timid openness to the world, outside the limits of the family environment. Through the different experiences lived, the adolescent is integrated into a group of equals, and it is in the late stage when their relationships with friends are consolidated, and their affective relationships seek more intimacy.
- Identity: in the search for their own identity, adolescents have different experiences going from the egocentric and fantasy world of children to a more abstract and realistic reasoning that allows them to establish clear objectives and limits and internalize their own moral, cultural, and social values.

Relationship changes

Our relationships, both friendship and romantic, expand our understanding of the world through new experiences and learning what it takes to care for others. As we get older, our reasons for making friendships change from what was important to us in our teen social lives. We start forming connections based on commonly shared ideas and values rather than overlapping activities. We also start enjoying the stability, intimacy, and support between our close friends over large groups.

Though many teens start dating in high school, during late adolescence, our romantic relationships become less about exploring sexuality and more about love and sharing personal experiences. Though we're still figuring out what we're looking for in our partners, "hook-up" culture can sometimes undermine our ability to learn the mutual support and openness it takes to keep up adult relationships. Ideally, we eventually find how to balance attraction, enjoyment, and respect to build the foundation for healthy relationships with the people we want to share our lives with.

Finding yourself as an adult

A lot of being a teenager is about testing out our identity as our minds and bodies go through big developmental changes. Late adolescence is when things start to stabilize, and we begin navigating life on our own terms for the first time.

We graduate high school and explore who we are in the world as many of us leave home, move to new cities, decide whether to go to college and start learning how to live on our own.

For better or worse, modern society's expectation no longer give us a clear path to adulthood.

It's up to us to figure out our new social roles as work and relationships norms keep changing. Many of our early morals come from things outside our control, like family traditions, peer approval, and school expectations.

During late adolescence, we get the chance to try new ideas for ourselves and sort through what we truly believe in. Figuring out what we value plays into our long-term choices and satisfaction. It provides the framework for big decisions, like if we need to weigh the trade-offs between the comfort of job security versus the risk of doing something we love.

As we take on new challenges and grow, we learn that mistakes are not reflections of self-worth, but rather more information that we can use toward giving us a sense of confidence in who we want to be. The last phase of growth we go through during late adolescence pushes us into an adventure of self-exploration.

# IV

Chapter 4: Parent's perspective

Being an Effective Parent:

What can I do to be a good parent for my early adolescent child?

Parents often become less involved in the lives of their children as they enter the middle grades. But your young adolescent needs as much attention and love from you as he needed when he was younger—and maybe more.

A good relationship with you or with other adults is the best safeguard your child has as he grows and explores. By the time he reaches adolescence, you and he will have had years of experience with each other; the parent of today's toddler is parent to tomorrow's teenager.

Your relationship with your child may change—in fact, it almost certainly must change—however, as she develops the skills required to be a successful adult.

These changes can be rewarding and welcome. As your middle school child makes mental and emotional leaps, your conversations will grow richer. As her interests develop and deepen, she may begin to teach you—how to slug a baseball, what is happening with the city council or county board or why a new book is worth reading.

America is home to people with a great variety of attitudes, opinions, and values. Americans have different ideas and priorities, which can affect how we choose to raise our children.

Across these differences, however, research has shown that being effective parents involves the following qualities:

★ Showing love: When our children behave badly, we may become angry or upset with them. We may also feel miserable because we become angry or upset. But these feelings are different from not loving our children. Young adolescents need adults who are there for them— people who connect with them, communicate with them, spend time with them and show a genuine interest in them. This is how they learn to care for and love others. According to school counsellor Carol Bleifield, "Parents can love their children but not necessarily love what they do—and children need to trust that this is true."

★ Providing support. Young adolescents need support as they struggle with problems that may seem unimportant to their parents and families. They need praise when they've done their best. They need encouragement to develop interests and personal characteristics.

★ Setting limits. Young adolescents need parents or other adults who consistently provide structure and supervision that is firm and appropriate for age and development. Limits keep all children, including young teens, physically and emotionally safe. Authoritarian parents who lay down hard-and-fast rules and expect their children to always do as they are told or permissive parents who have very few rules or regulations and give their children too much freedom are most likely to have the most difficult time as parents.

Their children are at risk for a range of negative behavioural and emotional consequences. However, authoritative parents, who set limits that are clear and come with explanations, tend to struggle less with their adolescents.

"Do it because I said so" probably didn't work for your son when he was 6 and it's even less likely to work now that he's an adolescent.

★ Being a role model. Young adolescents need strong role models. Try to live the behaviour and values that you hope your child will develop. Your actions speak louder than words. If you set high standards for yourself and treat others with kindness and respect, your child stands a better chance of following your example. As adolescents explore possibilities of who they may become, they look to their parents, peers, well-known personalities, and others to define who they may become.

★ Teaching responsibility. We are not born knowing how to act responsibly. A sense of responsibility is formed over time. As children grow up, they need to learn to take more and more responsibility for such things as:

—completing chores, such as doing yard work, cleaning their rooms, or helping to prepare meals, that contribute to the family's wellbeing.

—completing homework assignments without being nagged.

—taking on community activities.

—finding ways to be useful to others; and

—admitting to both the good and bad choices that they make.

★ Providing a range of experiences.

Adolescence is a time for exploring many areas and doing new things. Your child may try new sports and new academic pursuits and read new books. He may experiment with different forms of art, learn about different cultures and careers, and take part in community or religious activities. Within your means, you can open doors for your child. You can introduce him to new people and to new worlds. In doing so, you may renew in yourself long-ignored interests and talents, which also can set a good example for your child. Don't be discouraged when his interests change.

★ Showing respect.

It is tempting to label all young adolescents as being difficult and rebellious. But these youngsters vary as much as do children in any other age group. Your child needs to be treated with respect, which requires you to recognize and appreciate her differences and to treat her as an individual. Respect also requires you to show compassion by trying to see things from your child's point of view and to consider her needs and feelings. By treating your young adolescent with respect, you help her to take pleasure in good behaviour. There are no perfect parents. However, a bad decision or an "off" day (or week or month) isn't likely to have any lasting impact on your child. What's most important in being an effective parent is what you do over time.

Communication

How can I communicate better with my child?

Young adolescents often aren't great communicators, particularly with their parents and other adults who love them.

Emily Hutchison, a middle school teacher from Texas notes that young teens "often feel they can talk with anyone better than their parents—even wonderful parents." "They tend to be private," explains Patricia Lemons, a middle school teacher in New Mexico. "They don't necessarily want to tell you what they did at school today."

Many psychologists have found, however, that when parents know where their children are and what they are doing (and when the adolescent knows the parent knows, what psychologists call monitoring), adolescents are at a lower risk for a range of bad experiences, including drug, alcohol, and tobacco use; sexual behaviour and pregnancy; and delinquency and violence. The key, according to psychologists, is to be inquisitive but not interfering, working to respect your child's privacy as you establish trust and closeness.

It's easiest to communicate with a young teen if you established this habit when your child was little.

As school counsellor Carol Bleifield explains, "You don't suddenly dive in during the seventh grade and say, 'So what did you do with your friends on Friday night?'" But it's not impossible to improve communication when your child reaches early adolescence. Here are some tips:

★ Realize that no recipe exists for successful communication.

What works for getting one child to talk about what's important doesn't always work with another one. One middle school teacher and mother of two says her daughter is open and talkative; her son is quieter.

But because her son likes to listen to music, to write and to read, this mother often goes with him to a local bookstore. Here, in a place where he's comfortable, the son describes stories and book characters as a link to what he is thinking and feeling.

By listening to music with him and proofreading his writing when he's willing to let her this mother encourages her son to open.

★ Listen.

"You need to spend a lot of time not talking," suggests Diane Crim, a middle school teacher in Utah.

To listen means to avoid interrupting and it means to pay close attention.

This is best done in a quiet place with no distractions. It's hard to listen carefully if you're also trying to cook dinner or watch television.

Often just talking with your child about a problem or an issue helps to clarify things.

Sometimes the less you offer advice, the more your young teen may ask you for it. Listening can also be the best way to uncover a more serious problem that requires your attention

★ Create opportunities to talk.

To communicate with your child, you need to make yourself available. Young adolescents resist "scheduled" talks; they don't open when you tell them to, but when they want to. Some teens like to talk when they first get home from school. Others may like to talk at the dinner table or at bedtime. Some parents talk with their children in the car, preferably when the radio, tapes and CDs aren't playing. "I take my daughter toa mall—not the closer one, but the cooler one that is an hour and a half away," says a middle school teacher and mother. Many of the best conversations grow out of shared activities. "Parents try to grab odd moments and have this deep communication with their child," notes Sherry Tipps, an Arkansas teacher. "Then they are frustrated because it doesn't happen."

★ Talk over differences. Communication breaks down for some parents because they find it hard to manage differences with their child. It's often easiest to limit these differences when you have put in place clear expectations. If your 13-year-old daughter knows she's to be home by 9:30

p.m.—and if she knows the consequences for not meeting this curfew—the likelihood that she will be home on time increases. Differences of opinion are easier to manage when we recognize that these differences can provide important opportunities for us to rethink the limits and to negotiate new ones, a skill that is valuable for your child to develop. For example, when your daughter is 14, setting a later curfew for some occasions may be fine. Such negotiations are possible because of your child's growing cognitive skills and ability to reason and consider many possibilities and views.

Because she can consider that her curfew should be later the weekend than on school nights, your insistence that "it doesn't matter" will only create a conflict. When differences arise, telling your child your concerns firmly but calmly can prevent differences from becoming battles. Explaining why your child made or wants to make a poor choice is more constructive: "Dropping out of your algebra class will cut off lots of choices for you in the future. Some colleges won't admit you without two years of algebra, plus geometry and some trigonometry. Let's get you some help with algebra."

★ Avoid over-reacting. Responding too strongly can lead to yelling and screaming and it can shut down conversation. "Try to keep anxiety and emotions out of the conversation—then kids will open up," advises eighth-grade teacher Anne Jolly from Alabama. Instead of getting riled up, she says, "It's better to ask, 'What do you think about what you did? Let's talk about this.'" Middle school teacher Charles Summers adds, "Kids are more likely to be open if they look at you as somebody who is not going to spread their secrets or get extremely upset if they confess something to you. If your kid says, 'I've got to tell you something. Friday night I tried beer,' and you go off the deep end, your kid won't tell you again." At a time when they are already judging themselves critically, adolescents make themselves vulnerable when they open to parents. We know that the best way to encourage a behaviour is to reward it. If you are critical when your teenager talks to you, what he sees is that his openness gets punished rather than rewarded

★ Talk about things that are important to your young teen.

Different youngsters like to talk about different things. Some of the things they talk about may not seem important to you, but, as school counsellor Carol Bleifield explains, "With kids, sometimes it's like a different culture. You need to try to understand this, to put yourself in their place and time." She cautions against pretending to be excited about something that bores you. By asking questions and listening, however, you can show your child that you respect his feelings and opinions. Here are topics that generally interest young adolescents: —School. If you ask your child, "What did you do in school today?" she most likely will answer, "Nothing." Of course, you know that isn't true. By looking at your child's assignment book or reading notices sent home by the school, you will know that on Tuesday, your 10-year-old began studying animals in South America that are headed for extinction or that the homecoming football game is Friday night. With this information, you then can ask your child about specific classes or activities, which is more likely to start a conversation. —Hobbies and personal interests. If your child loves sports, talk about his favourite team, or event or watch the World Series or the Olympics with him. Most young adolescents are interested in music. Barbara Braithwaite, a middle school teacher in Pennsylvania notes that "Music has been the signature of every generation. It defines each age group. Parents ought to at least know the names of popular singers." It's important, however, to tell your child when you believe that the music, he is listening to is inappropriate—and to explain why. Your silence can be misconstrued as approval. —Emotions. As was pointed out earlier, young adolescents worry about a lot of different things. They worry about their friends, being popular, sexuality, being overweight or scrawny, tomorrow's math test, grades, getting into college, being abandoned and the future of the world. The list goes on. Sometimes it's hard to know if a problem seems big to your child. School counsellor Carol Bleifield says that if she is unsure, she asks, "Is this a small problem, a medium problem or a big problem? How important is it to you? How often do you worry about it?" Figuring out the size and importance of the problem helps her decide how to address it.

—Family.

Young adolescents like to talk about and be involved in plans for the whole family, such as vacations, as well as things that affect them individually, such as curfews or allowances. If you need back surgery, your child will want to know ahead of time. She may also want to learn more about the operation. Being a part of conversations about such topics can contribute to your child's feelings of belonging and security.

—Sensitive subjects.

Families should handle sensitive subjects in a way that is consistent with their values. Remember, though, that avoiding such subjects won't make them go away. If you avoid talking with your child about sensitive subjects, he may turn to the media or his friends for information. This increases the chances that what he hears will be out of line with your values or that the information will be wrong or both Sharon Sikora, a middle school teacher from Colorado, explains that middle schoolers have wrong or inaccurate information about many important subjects. They will say they know about certain sensitive topics, but they really don't. Discussing a sensitive subject directly may not work, Ms. Sikora notes, "You can't just sit down and say, 'Today we are going to talk about marijuana use.' That shuts down the conversation before you ever start."

—Parents' lives, hopes, and dreams.

Many young adolescents want a window to their parents' world, both past and present. How old were you when you got your ears pierced? Did you ever have a teacher who drove you crazy? Did you get an allowance when you were 11? If so, how much? Were you sad when your grandpa died? What is your boss like at work? This doesn't mean you are obligated to dump all your problems and emotions into your child's lap. You are a parent not a peer and an inappropriate question may best be left answered. However, recounting some things about your childhood and your life today can help your child sort out his own life.

—The future.

As the cognitive abilities of young adolescents develop, they begin to think more about the future and its possibilities. Your child may want to talk more about what to expect in the years to come life after high school, jobs, and marriage. He may ask questions such as, "What is it like to live in a college dormitory?" "How old do you have to be to get married?" "Is there any chance that the world will blow up some day?" "Will there be enough gasoline so that I can drive a car when I get older?" These questions deserve the best answers that you can provide (and those that you can't answer deserve an honest, "I don't know.").

—Culture, current events.

Ours is a media-rich world. Even young children are exposed to television, music, movies, video and computer games and other forms of media. Remember, though, that the media can provide a window into your adolescent's world. For example, if you and your child have seen the same movie (together or separately), you can ask her whether she liked it and what parts she liked best.

★ Communicate with kindness and respect. Young teens can say or do things that are outrageous or meanspirited or both. However hard your child pushes your buttons, it's best to respond calmly. The respect and self-control that you display in talks with your child may someday be reflected in her conversations with others. How you say something is as important as what you say. "Stop picking at your face" can reduce a young adolescent to tears. "Your room looks like a pigsty" isn't as helpful as, "You need to spend some time picking up your room. The job will be easier if you spend 5 minutes right now picking the clothes up off the floor—putting the dirty ones in the hamper and hanging the clean ones up. After lunch you can spend 5 minutes straightening up your bookshelf." Youngsters also pay attention to the tone of your voice. A 10-yearold can easily tell a calm voice from an angry one Kindness goes together with respect. As Joan Lipsitz, a nationally recognized authority on educating middle-grade students and the mother of two grown children, explains, "When I was an active parent and teacher, I had a rule that grew out of a classroom experience: 'I will never knowingly be unkind to you, and you will never knowingly be unkind to me.' That turned out to be the most powerful rule I ever set, either in the classroom—it changed the culture—or at home." Communicating with respect also requires not talking down to adolescents. They are becoming more socially conscious and aware of events in the world, and they appreciate thoughtful conversations. Jerri Foley, a middle school counsellor in South Carolina, tells the story of a trip she made with a group of adolescent girls when the state was debating whether to continue flying the Confederate battle flag from atop the state house. "We were driving along the highway when we got into a big discussion," she recalls. "We got so intense talking about it that we missed the exit to come home."

Independence

How much independence should I give to my child?

As children enter adolescence, they often beg for more freedom. Parents walk a tightrope between wanting their children to be confident and able to do things for themselves and knowing that the world can be a scary place with threats to their children's health and safety. Some parents allow too much of the wrong kind of freedom or they offer freedom before the adolescent is ready to accept it. Other parents cling too tightly, denying young teens both the responsibilities they require to develop maturity and the opportunities they need to make choices and accept their consequences. Research tells us that adolescents do best when they remain closely connected to their parents but at the same time are allowed to have their own points of view and even to disagree with their parents. Here are some tips to help balance closeness and independence:

★ Set limits.

All children sometimes resist limits, but they want them, and they need them. In a world that can seem too hectic for adults and adolescents alike, limits provide a security. Oftentimes, adolescents whose parents do not set limits feel unloved. Setting limits is most effective when it begins early. It is harder but not impossible, however, to establish limits during early adolescence

★ Be clear.

Most young teens respond best to specific instructions, which are repeated regularly. As middle school teacher Sharon Sikora notes, "Don't just say, 'I want your room clean,' because they don't know what that means. Say, in a non-argumentative way, 'This is how I perceive a clean room.' They may say, 'I don't really want the lamp over here, I want it over there.' Give them the freedom to express themselves."

★ Give reasonable choices.

Choices make young teens more open to guidance. For example, you can tell your son that his algebra homework must be done before bedtime, but that he has a choice of completing it either before or after supper. And you can tell your 14-year-old daughter that she can't hang around the video arcade with her friends on Saturday night, but she can have a group of friends over to your house to watch a movie. Using humour and creativity as you give choices may also make your child more willing to accept them. One middle school teacher couldn't get her own child to hang up clean clothes or put dirty clothes in the laundry basket. So, she gave her daughter two options

—either all the clothes had to be picked up or everything would go on the floor. "I was washing the clothes, then putting them in piles on the floor," the teacher recalls. "It made me crazy, but it worked." After two weeks, her daughter got tired of the stacks on the floor, and she began picking up her clothes.

★ Grant independence in stages.

The more mature and responsible a young teen's behaviour is, the more privileges parents can grant. You might first give your young teen the right to choose which sneakers to buy within a certain price range. Later you can let him make other clothing purchases—with the understanding that price tags won't be removed until you approve the items. Eventually, you can give him a clothing allowance to spend as he likes.

★ Health and safety come first.

Your most important responsibility as a parent is to protect your child's health and safety. Your child needs to know that your love for her requires you to veto activities and choices that threaten either of these. Let your child know what things threaten her health and safety

—and often the health and safety of others

—and put your foot down. Doing this is made more difficult, though, because adolescents have a sense that nothing can hurt them. While he feels that everything, he experiences is new and unique, an adolescent also believes that what happens to others will not happen to him. His beliefs are since adolescence is the healthiest period during our lives. In this period, physical illnesses are not common and fatal disease is rare. The important thing to emphasize to your child is that, while he may be very healthy, death and injury during adolescence are most often caused by violence and accident

★ Say no to choices that cut off future options.

Some things aren't worth fighting about. It may offend you if your son wears a shirt to school that clashes wildly with his pants, but this isn't a choice that can cut off future possibilities for him. Young teens may have a growing sense of the future, but they still lack the experiences required to fully understand how a decision they make today can affect them tomorrow. They may have heard that smoking is unhealthy, but they do not fully understand what it means to die of lung cancer at the age of 45. Talk to your children about the lifelong consequences of choices they make. Help them understand there are good and bad decisions and that knowing one from the other can make all the difference in their lives. Let your child know that you are "the keeper of options" until he is old enough and responsible enough to assume this responsibility: He may not skip school and he may not avoid taking tough courses that will prepare him for college.

★ Guide but resist the temptation to control.

The earlier section on being an effective parent discussed the importance of striking a good balance between laying down the law and allowing too much freedom. With most young teens, it's easiest to maintain this balance by guiding but not controlling. Young teens need opportunities to explore different roles, try on new personalities and experiment. They need to learn that choices have consequences. That means making some mistakes and accepting the results. But parents need to provide guidance so that young teens avoid making too many poor choices. You can guide by being a good listener and by asking questions that help your child to think about the results of her actions: "What could happen if you let someone who is drunk drive you home?" Your guidance may be better appreciated if you ask your child's advice on a range of matters and follow the advice if it seems reasonable: "What should we cook for Daddy's birthday?" "I don't have to work on Saturday. Is there anything special you'd like to do?" The fine line between guiding and controlling may be different for different children. Some children, whether they are 7 or 17, need firmer guidance and fewer privileges than do other children at the same age. One middle school teacher explains how the different behaviour of her own two teens created a need for different limits: "My daughter understood a midnight curfew to mean that she either had to be in the house with the door locked by 12 or else she must have placed the call from the emergency room informing her parents that she had broken her leg. My son, who was 15 months younger, understood a midnight curfew to mean that he could call at 11:59 p.m. to inform his parents that he'd be home after the pizza he'd ordered with his buddies had arrived and been consumed and he'd driven home his 6 friends."

★ Let kids make mistakes. We want our children to grow into adults who can solve problems and make good choices. These abilities are a critical part of being independent. To develop these abilities, however, young teens on occasion may need to fail, provided the stakes aren't too high and no one's health or safety is at risk. Making mistakes also allows young teens to learn one critical skill—how to bounce back. It's hard for a child to learn how to pick himself up and start over if his parents always rescue him from difficulties.

★ Make actions have consequences.

If you tell your child that she must be home by 10 p.m., do not ignore her midnight arrival. You lose credibility with your child if she suffers no consequences for returning home two hours late. However, the punishment should fit the crime. Grounding a child for six weeks restricts the entire family. Instead, you might talk with your child about how coming in two hours late has affected you. You've been up worrying and have missed your sleep. But you'll still have to get up the next morning at your regular time, make breakfast, do your chores, and go to work. Because her lack of consideration has made your life harder, she will have to complete some of your chores so that you can get to bed earlier the next night. Finally, and despite what we often hear and read, adolescents look to their parents first and foremost in shaping their lives. When it comes to morals and ethics, political beliefs and religion, teenagers almost always have more in common with their parents than their parents believe. As a parent, you should look beyond the surface, beyond the specific behaviours to who your child is becoming. Your teenager may want to dye her hair purple and pierce most parts of her body, but these expressions may be independent of her sense of who she is and who she will become. While many of your child's behaviours are ultimately harmless, some of them may not only be harmful but also deadly. Parents need to talk to their children and make it clear that many of the major threats to their future health and happiness are not a matter of chance but are a matter of choice—choices like drinking and driving, smoking, drugs, sexual activity, and dropping out of school.

Confidence

How can I help my child to become more confident?

Young teens often feel inadequate. They have new bodies and developing minds and their relationships with friends and family members are in flux. They understand for the first time that they aren't good at everything. The changes in their lives may take place more rapidly than their ability to adjust to them. Poor self-esteem often peaks in early adolescence, then improves during the middle and late teen years as identities gain strength and focus.

At any age, however, a lack of confidence can be a serious problem. Young teens with poor self-esteem can be lonely, awkward with others and sensitive to criticism and with what they see as their shortcomings. Young teens with low confidence are less likely to join in activities and form friendships. This isolates them further and slows their ability to develop a better self-image. When they do make friends, they are more vulnerable to negative peer pressure. Some young adolescents who lack confidence hold back in class. Others act out to gain attention.

At its worst, a lack of confidence is often linked with self-destructive behaviour and habits—smoking or drug or alcohol use, for example. Girls often experience deeper self-doubts than do boys (although there are many exceptions).

This can be for many reasons:

★ Society sends girls the message that it is important for them to get along with others and to be very, very thin, and pretty. Life can be just as hard, however, for a boy who thinks he must meet society's expectations that boys have to be good at sports and other physical activities.

★ Girls mature physically about two years earlier than do boys, which requires girls to deal with issues of how they look, popularity and sexuality before they are emotionally mature enough to do so. ★ Girls may receive confusing messages about the importance of achievement. Although girls are told that achievement is important, some also fear that they won't be liked, especially by boys, if they come across as too smart or too capable, especially in the areas of math, science, and technology. If your young adolescent suffers from a severe lack of confidence over long period, she may benefit from seeing a counsellor or other professional. This is especially true if she also has a drug or alcohol problem, a learning disability, an eating disorder, or severe depression. Most young adolescents will get through the rough spots with adequate time and support. For example, adolescents may think about several situations: competing on the track team, studying math, dating, taking care of younger brothers or sisters and so on. An adolescent is likely to feel more confident doing some of these things than others. She may feel very good about her athletic ability and skill at math but feel bad about her dating life. She may also have mixed feelings about how good a sister she is to her baby brother. How good this teenager feels about herself ties to how important each of these areas is to her. If having a very active dating life is the most important area of her life, this girl will feel bad about herself. If being a scholar-athlete is most important area, then she will feel very good about herself. Based on this theory, the best ways to help your child to develop confidence include the following:

★ Provide opportunities for your child to succeed. As teacher Diane Crim points out, "The best way to instil confidence in someone is to give them successful experiences. You need to set them up to succeed—give them experiences where they can see how powerful they are. Kids can engineer those experiences. Part of confidence is knowing what to do when you don't know what to do." Help your child to build confidence in his abilities by encouraging him to take an art class, act in a play, join a soccer or baseball team, participate in science fairs or computer clubs, or play a musical instrument—whatever he likes to do that brings out the best in him. Don't push a particular activity on your child. Most children, whether they are 3 or 13 years old, resist efforts to get them to do things that they don't enjoy. Pushing children to participate in activities they haven't chosen for themselves can lead to frustration. Try to balance your child's experiences between activities that he is already good at doing with new activities or with activities that he is not so good at doing. You can also help your child to build confidence by assigning him family responsibilities at which he can succeed—unloading the dishwasher, cleaning his room, or mowing the lawn.

★ Help young teens feel safe and trust in themselves. The ability of adolescents to trust in themselves comes from receiving unconditional love that helps them to feel safe and to develop the ability to solve their own problems. Your child, like all children, will encounter situations that require her to lean on you and others. But always relying on you to bail her out of tough situations can stunt her emotional growth. "We have to teach our children how to cope with the things they encounter, instead of easing the path," says teacher Anne Jolly.

★ Talk about anxieties that are related to school violence and to global terrorism. Many children have seen terrifying images of death and destruction on television and on the Internet. You can help your child to understand that although the country has suffered awful acts of terror, we are strong people who can come together and support each other through difficult times. In addition, you can: —Create a calm environment in your home through your own behaviour. This may not be possible if your family has been affected directly by an act of terror or violence. If you are anxious, you need to explain to your child what you are feeling and why. Children take emotional cues from those they love. —Listen to what your child has to say. Assure him that adults are working to make homes and schools safe. —Help your child to separate fact from fiction. Discuss facts with your child and avoid guessing, exaggerating, or overreacting. —Monitor your child's television, radio, and Internet activity. Help her to avoid overexposure to violent images, which can heighten her anxiety. —Use historical examples (for example, Pearl Harbours or the Challenger space shuttle explosion) to explain to your child that bad things happen to innocent people, but that people go on with their lives and resolve even terrible situations. —Continue your normal family routines

★ Praise and encourage. Praise is meaningful to adolescents when it comes from those they love and count on most—their parents and other important adults in their lives. Praising your child will help her to gain confidence. However, the compliments that you give her must be genuine. She will recognize when they are not.

★ Have patience. As adults, most people have confidence. This confidence comes about through years of experiencing success, but also through years of exploring strengths and weakness and choosing to stress different parts of our lives. Most of us would be unhappy if we had to do only those things that we are not good at. As adults, we tend to find our areas of strength and—to the extent we can—to pursue these areas more than others. For an adolescent, however, it is difficult to downplay the areas in which they are less confident. For example, it is very hard for an adolescent with academic skills to focus on school rather than on dating, when all her friends are dating and telling her how important dating is. For a parent this can lead to feelings of helplessness. You know that whether that cute new boy asked out your daughter will have little consequence on her life for the long run, but you also know that she cannot yet see this!

How can I help my child to form good friendships and to resist harmful peer pressure?

Friendships can affect many areas of young adolescents' lives—grades, how they spend their time, what clubs they join and how they behave in public places, such as a shopping mall. Youngsters who have trouble forming friendships are more likely to have poor self-esteem, do poorly in school, drop out, get involved in delinquent behaviour and suffer from a range of psychological problems as adults. Children of all ages need to feel that they fit in— that they belong. As children approach the teen years, the need to be "one of the gangs" is stronger than at any other age. Friendships become closer and more important and play a key part in allowing young adolescents to sort out who they are and where they're headed. They are likely to form small groups or cliques, each with a special identity (for example, jocks, brains, preppies, or geeks). Many parents worry that their children's friends will become so influential in their lives that their own roles will diminish. Parents worry still more that their children's friends will encourage them to take part in harmful activities.

The peak period for peer influence is generally from seventh to ninth grades. During this time, friends often influence taste in music, clothes, or hairstyles, as well as the activities in which youngsters choose to participate. However, peers do not replace parents. You are still the most important influence in your child's life. Young teens are more inclined to turn to their parents than to peers for guidance in deciding what post high-school plans to make, what career to select and what religious and moral values to choose. This influence is greatest when the bond between parent and child is strong.

Here are some tips to guide you in helping your child to form good friendships:

★ Recognize that peer pressure can be bad or good. Most young teens are drawn to friends who are like them. If your child chooses friends who are not interested in school and who make poor grades, he may be less willing to study or complete assignments. If he chooses friends who like school and do well in their studies, however, his motivation to get good grades may be strengthened. Friends who avoid alcohol and drugs also will exert a positive influence on your child.

★ Get to know your child's friends. A good way to learn about your child's friends is to drive them to events—talking with them in the car can reveal a lot. You can also welcome your child's friends into your home. Make it a place with food and a comfortable atmosphere. Having your child's friends at your home can provide you with peace of mind and allow you to set the rules of conduct, as well as help you to gain a better understanding of what they talk about and what their concerns are.

★ Get to know the parents of your child's friends. You don't have to be best buddies, but it helps to know if other parents' attitudes and approaches to parenting are like yours. Former principal Carole Kennedy explains, "The kid may seem okay, but you need to know if someone is around at the other house to supervise." Knowing the other parent makes it easier to learn what you need to know: where your child is going, who she's going with, what time the activity starts and ends, whether an adult will be present and how your child will get to and from the activity.

★ Provide your child with some unstructured time in a safe place to hang around with friends. Activities are important, but too many piano lessons or basketball practices can lead to burnout. Allowing your child some unstructured time with friends in a safe place with adult supervision lets him share ideas and develop important social skills. For example, among friends your child can learn that good friends are good listeners, that they are helpful and confident (but not overly so), that they are enthusiastic, possess a sense of humour and that they respect others. Spending time with others may also help your child to change some behaviours that make others uncomfortable around him: being too serious or unenthusiastic, critical of others or too stubborn.

★ Talk with your child about friends, about friendship and about making choices. It's normal for adolescents to care about what others think of them. This makes it especially important for you to talk with your youngster about resisting the pressure to disobey the rules or go against the standards and values that she has been taught. You can talk with her about how to be a good friend and about how all friendships have their ups and downs. You can also talk about the importance of making good choices when she is with friends. "I always tell them, 'If it feels wrong, it probably is,'" explains teacher Barbara Braithwaite. Teacher Charles Summers tells his middle school students and his own children, "You need to look at who you are when you are with this person." He also suggests that they ask themselves this question: "How do you want to be described by others?" Children's responses can guide their behaviour.

★ Teach your child how to get out of a bad situation. Talk with your child about dangerous or inappropriate situations that might arise and about possible ways to handle them. Ask your 14-year-old daughter what she would do if a guest arrived at a slumber party with a bottle of wine in her overnight bag. Ask your 12-year-old son how he would handle a suggestion from a friend to cut school and head for a nearby burger place. Ideally, youngsters themselves can be the ones to say "no" to a potentially dangerous or destructive situation. But if they haven't yet learned this skill, parent Marianne Cavanaugh from Connecticut suggests an alternative: "Sometimes kids don't want to do what their peers want them to do. I tell my kids to blame me—to tell their friends that their mom says 'no.' This helps get them off the hook." Finally, no child going out for an evening should be without change for a phone call. As a last resort, this may be his lifeline. A cell phone may also be appropriate if family finances allow one and if the child knows how to use the phone responsibly.

★ Monitor friendships to help your child avoid risky and unhealthy behaviour. Young adolescents need supervision, including during the important after-school hours. Keep tabs on who your child's friends are and what they do when they get together. Bill Gangl, a middle school teacher in Minnesota, suggests, "Don't be afraid to be the jerk who makes the phone call to the other house to make sure that (your child) is there. And don't be afraid to say no." Many middle school teachers and parents have different opinions as to whether parents can or should try to stop their children from seeing a friend that the parents dislike. Some youngsters will rebel if told they can't spend time with certain friends. Many adults who have worked with young teens suggest that you let your child know that you disapprove of a friendship and why you disapprove. They also suggest that you limit the amount of time and the activities that you will allow with the friend.

★ Model good friendships. The example of friendship you provide has a bigger impact on your child's friendships than any lecture. Children who see their parents treat each other and their friends with kindness and respect have an advantage. Baking cookies for the new neighbour or offering a listening ear for an unhappy friend sends your child a powerful message.

What can I do to keep the media from being a bad influence on my child?

It's hard to understand the world of early adolescents without considering the huge impact on their lives of the mass media. It competes with families, friends, schools, and communities in its ability to shape young teens' interests, attitudes, and values. The mass media infiltrates their lives. Most young adolescents watch TV and movies, surf the Internet, exchange e-mails, listen to CDs and to radio stations that target them with music and commercials and read articles and ads in teen magazines. First, look on the bright side. The new media technologies can be fun and exciting. Used wisely, they can also educate. Good TV programs can inform, good music can comfort, and good movies can expand interests and unlock mysteries. Additionally, many forms of media are being used in classrooms today—computers, cable-equipped TVs and VCRs are all part of the landscape. Indeed, recent years have seen a commitment to connecting every classroom to the Internet and providing a reasonable number of computers to each classroom for student use. As a result, children need to be exposed to media, if only to learn how to use it.

The problem is that young adolescents often don't—or can't—distinguish between what's good in the media and what's bad. Some spend hours in front of the TV or plugged into earphones, passively taking in what they see and hear—violence, sex, profanities, stereotyping and story lines and characters that are unrealistic. We know from research such as that conducted by George Comstock and Erica Sherrar that seeing too much TV violence appears to increase aggressive behaviour in children and that regular viewing of violence makes violence less shocking and more acceptable. Students who report watching the most TV have lower grades and lower test scores than do those who watch less TV. "In any classroom discussion I have, it is very apparent who's watching [a lot of] television and who's not," explains teacher Sherry Tipps. "For the kids who are not motivated in the classroom, mention TV and suddenly they perk up." As young teens mature, high levels of TV-viewing, videogame playing, and computer use take their toll. On average, American children spend far more time with the media than they do completing work for school. Seventh graders, for example, spend an average of 135 minutes each day watching TV and 57 minutes doing schoolwork.

★ Limit the amount of time your child spends viewing TV. It's impossible to protect your child entirely from the media. Banning TV entirely may only strengthen its appeal to her. However, some parents do make TV viewing off-limits during the school week, except for special programs that are agreed to ahead of time. Remember, it's easier to restrict your child's poor media choices if you say no before she brings home the objectionable CDs or computer games or turns on the violent TV programs. Let your child know that you will monitor her media choices.

★ Monitor what your child watches and listens to. Former principal Carole Kennedy advises, "Don't just listen to how loud the music is, but to what the words are." Learn about the TV programs and movies that your child wants to watch, the computer games he wants to play and the music he wants to listen to. Knowing something about your child's interests will let you enter his world and talk with more knowledge and force about his choices. Ask your young teen what bands or singers he likes. Then read about his favourites in magazines or newspapers or listen to their CDs or to the radio stations that play their music.

★ You can also watch or listen with your child. This allows you to spend time with him and to learn more about the programs, games, and music that he likes. Talk with your child about what you are seeing and hearing.

★ Suggest TV programs that you want your child to watch. Encourage your child to watch TV programs about a variety of subjects—nature, travel, history, science, biography, and news, as well as programs that entertain. News and history programs, for example, can encourage conversations about world issues, national and local politics, social problems, and health concerns.

★ Talk with your child about the difference between facts and points of view. Young teens need to learn that not everything they hear or see is true. Let your child know that the TV show or movie he sees, the radio station or music he listens to and the magazine he reads may have a definite point of view. Talk with him about how the media can promote certain ideas or beliefs, which may be different from those of your family. If your child wants to watch, listen to, or read something that you believe is inappropriate, let him know exactly why you object. ★ Talk with your child about misleading ads. Young adolescents are especially vulnerable to advertising. Talk with your child about what ads are for—to sell products—and about how to judge whether the products the ads sell are right for her. If, for example, your daughter has short, blond, curly hair, ask her if she really thinks the shampoo that she wants you to spend $15 for will make her hair look like the long, black, straight hair on the model in the magazine ad.

★ Consider buying a V-chip for your TV or a filter for your computer. A V-chip is a computer chip that can detect program ratings—X, R, PG and so on and so block your child from watching pornographic, violent, or other inappropriate TV channels. Similar chips or filters can prevent your child from visiting certain Web sites. Many of these can be obtained for free or for modest costs at your local electronics store.

★ Talk with your child about the risks of visiting computer chat rooms. Let your child know the dangers of "talking" online with strangers. There is software that can restrict children from chat rooms, even as they allow access to other content.

★ Talk with other parents. Discussing movies, TV shows, computer games and CDs with the parents of your child's friends and classmates can give you more strength to say no when she wants to see or hear something that think is inappropriate. You also can quickly find out that not everyone in the seventh grade is going to be allowed to see the latest R-rated movie in which bloody bodies are strewn across the screen.

★ Provide alternatives to media entertainment. According to teacher Bill Gangl, "If you give the kids enough activities, the TV goes away." Given the opportunity, many children would rather do than watch. A day at a miniature golf course or a visit with a friend may hold more appeal for your child than watching TV.

★ Model alternative forms of entertainment. A young teen whose parent is constantly in front of the TV or checking her e-mail over a quick dinner is being sent a definite message. Parents who turn off the TV or computer and engage in conversation, sports, games, or other activities are showing alternatives to their children. An adolescent today may well wonder "what did you do before TV (or computers or video games)?" Show them!

What can I do to help my child to develop good values and to learn right from wrong?

We want our children to develop respect and compassion for others. We want them to be honest, decent, and thoughtful—to stand up for their principles, to cooperate with others and to act responsibly. We want them to make sound moral choices. The payoffs for encouraging a child's values are enormous: those who grow up with strong, consistent, and positive values are happier, do better in school and are more likely to contribute to society. Talk to your children about good values and why they matter. Just as children need to be guided academically, so too must they be educated in the values of a civil society—values like love your neighbour; give an honest day's work for an honest day's wages; tell the truth and be honest; respect others, respect their property and respect their opinions; and take responsibility for your decisions. In word and deed, parents play an important role in helping their children develop a good sense of right from wrong and good from bad. Many of the major threats to our children today are not a matter of chance but are a matter of choice—choices like drinking and driving, smoking, drugs, sex, and dropping out of school.

★ When your daughter senses that her parents appreciate people of all colours and creeds, she is likely to become more open to friends of all races and backgrounds.

★ When you tell a salesclerk that she gave you change for a ten-dollar bill and not a five, your child sees honesty in action.

★ When your child sees his parents make tough choices— "We're buying a used car so that we can save more money for a vacation"—he picks up the cues.

★ If you accept disappointments as a part of life—if you pick yourself up and keep going—your child stands a better chance of becoming a survivor.

★ If you can laugh at your own mistakes, your child is more likely to accept his own imperfections.

★ When you volunteer at a food kitchen, your child will be more likely to have compassion for others who are less fortunate. The way that you view money and material goods can also mold your child's attitudes. If you see your self-worth and the worth of others in terms of cars, homes, furniture, nice clothes and other possessions, your child is more likely to develop these attitudes as well. It is equally important to meet your child's needs but to guide him to set them apart from his wants. The expensive leather jacket that he must have may be OK—if you can afford it. Giving your child an allowance is one good way to help her understand the value of money. But you must decide how much the allowance will be, considering your resources, your child's age, and what expenses the allowance will cover (lunches, clothes, church donations, entertainment or whatever). An allowance can help your young teen learn how to save and how to use money wisely. Naturally, parents want to disclose information and provide guidance that is consistent with their values and religious beliefs. We know from child development experts that parents are often better at providing information about the facts of life than they are at talking about what matters more: their values concerning sexuality. To make good decisions, young teens need to have accurate information about "the birds and the bees" that takes into consideration strong values. Parents often find it easier to teach their children values when they rely on their friends and other parents for support and guidance. Many parents also draw support from their churches, synagogues, mosques, or other religious institutions. At some point in their adolescent-rearing efforts, many parents find themselves disappointed and frustrated. ("I can't believe my kid did something so dumb and insensitive. What did I do wrong?") Generally, there is no reason to panic if your child sometimes behaves in a way that differs from your standards—if he doesn't do it regularly. Bad behaviour needs to be recognized and dealt with. But we would all do well to remember our own adolescence—most of us turned out OK.

Alcohol or Drug Use

Because early adolescence can be a confusing and stressful time for children, it is not surprising that this is the time when many of them first try alcohol, tobacco, and other drugs. Because mood swings and unpredictable behaviour are common among young teens, parents often find it hard to spot signs of alcohol and drug abuse. If your child starts to show some of the following signs, drugs or alcohol may be at the heart of the problem –

★ He's withdrawn, depressed, tired, and careless about personal grooming.

★ She's hostile and uncooperative and often breaks curfews.

★ He has new friends (and may not want to talk about them).

★ She doesn't want to tell you where she is going and what she is going to do.

★ His grades slip.

★ She's lost interest in hobbies, sports and other activities that were once favourites.

★ His eating or sleeping patterns have changed; he's up late at night and sleeps during the day.

★ Her relationship with family members has worsened and she refuses to discuss school, activities, friends, or other important subjects.

Eating Disorder

Eating orders usually occur in females. Eating disorders in males are usually associated with athletics, especially wrestling.

The most common eating disorders are anorexia nervosa and bulimia.

Anorexia is an emotional disorder that can be signalled by severe weight loss or failure to gain weight.

About 90 percent of the people who have this disorder are females. Studies suggest that one in 250 young women may suffer from anorexia, with symptoms most often first appearing in early to middle adolescence. Bulimia can be signalled by episodes of binge eating followed by self-induced vomiting, fasting or strenuous exercise. Bulimia tends to develop among older adolescents, many of whom have also been anorexic. Many physical disorders are associated with eating disorders, such as kidney problems, irregular heart rhythms, irritation, and tears in the esophagus, dizziness or fainting and stomach and intestinal problems. The death rate is from 5 to 15 percent, but it is lower if sufferers receive treatment.

Take your worries to an expert if your child:

★ loses a large amount of weight for no medical reason.

★ reduces the amount of food she eats and/or stops eating high carbohydrate and fatty foods.

★ exercises excessively despite weakness and fatigue.

★ possesses an intense fear of gaining weight.

★ stops menstruating.

★ binges on foods that are high in calories; or

★ tries to control her weight by vomiting or using laxatives or diuretics.

Depression and Suicide

An increase in suicides among young adolescents makes it vital for parents to recognize the causes and symptoms. Many factors can contribute to serious depression that can lead to suicide. If a parent suffers from extreme depression, a child is more likely to experience it, too. But situations such as broken or unhappy families, the loss of parent through divorce or death, sexual abuse or drug or alcohol abuse may also contribute to depression. Other stressful situations may also play a role: for example, losing a relative, being ignored by friends or serious concerns about sexuality.

Some warning signs of depression and possible suicidal tendencies include:

★ Change in sleeping patterns (either sleeping too much or too little).

★ Change in behaviour (can't concentrate on school, work, or routine tasks, slipping grades).

★ Change in personality (seems sad, withdrawn, irritable, anxious, tired, indecisive, apathetic).

★ Change in eating habits (loss of appetite and weight or overeating).

★ Physical changes, (including a lack of energy, sudden weight gain or loss, lack of interest in appearance).

★ A major loss or life change (through death, divorce, separation, broken relationship).

★ Decreased interest in friends, school, or activities.

★ Low self-esteem (feeling worthless, overwhelming guilt, self-hatred).

★ No hope for the future (believes things will never get better, that nothing will ever change)

★ Preoccupation with music, art, and personal writing about death; ★ Giving away prized possessions and otherwise "getting affairs in order;" and

★ Direct suicide threats or comments such as, "I wish I was dead!" "My family would be better off without me." or "I don't have anything to live for." These threats should always be taken seriously

## Conclusion

No one can guarantee that young adolescents will grow into responsible and competent adults. Your influence on your young teen, however, is enormous. Yes, on a bad day the smelly sneakers and mood swings may push you to your limits. But it is critical to remain involved. It's when you are ready to throw up your hands in frustration that you most need to hang in. Learning as much as you can about the world of early adolescents is an important step toward helping your child—and you—through the fascinating, confusing, and wonderful years. As middle school teacher Emily Hutchison from Texas puts it, early adolescence is "never dull, never boring." Stay tuned to the life of your young teen and enjoy this special time.

9 798885 912020

Printed by Libri Plureos GmbH in Hamburg,
Germany